BRIDGERTON'S BATH

CONTENTS

INTRODUCTION

Bridgerton made its sensational debut in December 2020. Adapting Julia Quinn's best-selling novels was a task that Shonda Rhimes had handed to Executive Producer Chris Van Dusen three years earlier and the result was Netflix's most popular original series.

'With *Bridgerton*, you get a daring take on love and relationships in 19th-century London, but you also get everything that comes along with being a Shondaland show,' says Van Dusen. 'These are smart, funny, tortured characters figuring out who they are.'

Apart from innovation in scripting and casting, *Bridgerton* pushed the envelope in every department, including musical arrangement, some vivid costume design and, most noticeable of all, some breathtaking location choices. London was too noisy and Victorian for street scenes – Bath was beautiful, Georgian, and the mellow Bath stone was a perfect fit for the production design. Bath stone *was* used in London buildings – the Duke of York used it to build Lancaster House, a rival to Buckingham Palace in elegance and opulence, making it the perfect location for some of *Bridgerton's* London scenes.

In choosing Bath for 14 locations Chris Van Dusen wasn't playing it safe either. The city is already one of the country's top tourist destinations and so shooting scenes less than a hundred yards from Bath Abbey (Modiste, Covent Garden) was not taking the easy path.

So, gentle reader, to give you the perfect excuse to bask in one more watch, we have taken all the major Bath locations that were used across the eight episodes and arranged them into a walking tour. Once you've experienced them on the ground, the immediate delight is to go back through the episodes and spot them again.

ABOVE LEFT
Chris Van Dusen is the taller of the duo standing outside Elton House, of which Modiste is a retail tenant.

LEFT
'Too many balls Your Grace?' Simon Basset, the Duke of Hastings is coaxed into attending another, as part of the grand ruse.

Bath is a city full of fascinating museums and none more relevant than No.1 Royal Crescent, where you can step back in time to experience the real Georgian period, both upstairs and downstairs. The Assembly Rooms, run today by the National Trust, were frequented by Jane Austen during her four years in Bath, while the queen of Regency romance took breakfasts at the Sydney Hotel, opposite her residence at 4, Sydney Place. But for the true *Bridgerton* fan there is nothing like the vicarious thrill of standing on the spot outside Gunter's tea room where Simon gave Daphne some devastating news, or stepping into the Abbey Deli for a reviving infusion in Madame Delacroix's wood-panelled fitting room of Modiste. And when you are finished, the rest of this inspiring city awaits you.

 # ROYAL CRESCENT

Bath's Royal Crescent is the perfect backdrop for many of the street scenes in Bridgerton

The Royal Crescent is a fine place to promenade, pick up the latest Whistledown, or take a carriage ride in one's own liveried coach. Bath has eight crescents but Royal Crescent is the largest and finest. The legacy of John Wood the Younger, it was built between 1767 and 1774 and is one of the best examples of Palladian architecture in Britain and Ireland. The John Wood father-and-son architectural partnership shaped Bath by their shared design vision and enthusiasm for the city. Passionate about returning Bath to its Roman roots, John Wood the Elder planned a forum, circus and gymnasium. His plans were changed but his vision remains in his designs for the nearby Circus. The Wood family trademark remains to this day, that of imposing terraces of grand townhouses looking like impressive country homes, in abeautifully landscaped setting. Typically, a Bath house has a Welsh slate roof, stone façade, elegant

sash windows and a large wooden front door; in the case of the Royal Crescent, all painted white.

There are 30 townhouses in the crescent, bookended by two grand mansions at No.1 and No.30. Today, No.1 is a museum with rooms set up as they would have looked in the Georgian era between 1777 and 1796. At the centre of the crescent is No.16 which today is the Royal Bath Spa hotel – five-star accommodation and virtually the same view that John Wood gazed out on in 1774.

BATH STONE

Bath is a city made of stone, thanks in no small part to Ralph Allen, a self-made man who became the city's mayor in 1742. After arriving in Bath from Cornwall aged 17, in 1710, he started work as a postal clerk and by the age of 19 he had risen to

ABOVE
Two of the beautifully dressed supporting artists, strolling along the Crescent.

ABOVE LEFT
A photo to delight the Curator of No.1 Museum, Amy Frost: 'It's always an absolute treat seeing the Royal Crescent empty of parked cars and free of traffic, but seeing it with wonderfully dressed people promenading and horses and carriages was brilliant.'

LEFT
Daphne and Colin's stunt doubles race across the cobbles in an attempt to stop the duel. In Regency times, Putney Heath and Wimbledon Common were popular London duelling grounds.

postmaster. Allen was a prodigious talent in the postal business and went on to reorganise the service in Bath and much of Great Britain. He used his profits to buy the quarries at Combe Down where limestone was excavated. Much of the stone used in buildings around the city comes from Allen's quarries. Working with architect John Wood he continued to subsidise the quarries when they failed to break even, thus continuing the supply to builders and helping give the city such a wealth of complementary buildings.

Bath Stone was rejected for building Sir Christopher Wren's Greenwich Hospital in London because it was considered too soft. However, Allen was keen to show off its qualities and used it to build his country home, Prior Park, just outside Bath. It was also shipped to Westminster to construct what would be London's largest private residence, York House (today Lancaster House and widely used in *Bridgerton*). King George III's second son, Prince Frederick, the Duke of York and Albany, started the project in 1825. He had been the second resident of No.1 The Crescent in 1776, and obviously liked the stone. It was his short occupancy of No.1 that transformed The Crescent into The Royal Crescent.

LEFT
One of Whistledown's hardworking delivery boys at work on the Crescent, in this case actor Nathan Vidal.

OPPOSITE
An aerial view of the Royal Crescent with the Circus to the right, the Assembly Rooms adjacent to the Circus on the right, and Gay Street stretching from the Circus downhill towards Queen Square.

BELOW
The composer Haydn thought the Royal Crescent 'magnificent'. It is said to have been inspired by the colonnade surrounding Rome's Piazza San Pietro.

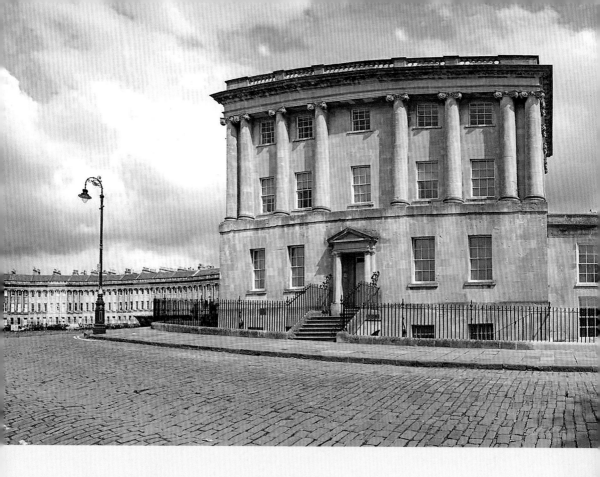

NO.1 ROYAL CRESCENT

The Featherington's Grosvenor Square house can be found at the end of the Royal Crescent

When it was completed in 1772 the Royal Crescent was deemed to be the perfect expression of Palladian architecture and No.1 is the grand residence that anchors the eastern end. From here the Featherington family emerge into Grosvenor Square to conduct their daily business in London. Over the years it has had many distinguished residents, including Prince Frederick, Duke of York and Albany.

Today it is a museum and HQ of the Bath Preservation Trust. In the past the house had been split off from its servants' wing at 1A, but in 2012, during an extensive restoration project, the two were reunited to give an insight into life 'above stairs' and 'below stairs'. Amy Frost, No.1 Museum's curator, believes there would have been a core of four servants: housekeeper/cook, a butler/footman, scullery maid and a footboy. 'Some households in taking the house may have had more, including personal servants. And staffing would have been a mixture of those who came with the occupants, those that

ABOVE
On screen, No.1 has added lampposts, stone lions, wall plaques and a balcony.

RIGHT
An adapted sedan chair sits outside the museum, which has ten Georgian rooms open to the public.

OPPOSITE
A tale of two drawing rooms: No.1 Museum's recreated Withdrawing Room (1780s) and the Featherington's slightly later version (1813).

came with the house and those hired in from Bath.'

Although Royal Crescent was originally the grandest development in Bath, it soon had its rivals: 'By the time of the Regency period (1795–1837) Great Pulteney Street had been developed, as had Lansdown Crescent, and although Royal Crescent continued to be the grandest address, the later houses of the 1780s–90s in those developments are actually larger. So by the time of the Regency period they were slightly more fashionable, if not quite as famous.' None of the houses in the Crescent were big enough to have their own ballroom, but Amy Frost says they could adapt if necessary: 'Large drawing rooms have doors separating them from the rear parlour, so that if the door were opened up for parties, dancing could take place with 2–5 couples.'

BATH ASSEMBLY ROOMS

Lady Danbury's ball was filmed in the Tea Room at Bath's historic Assembly Rooms

The Assembly Rooms were the venue in Bath where high society met for concerts and balls. It was a place to see and be seen, for games of cards, small theatrical events and, most of all, gossip. Jane Austen knew them well and incorporated scenes at the Assembly Rooms into her classic novels *Persuasion* and *Northanger Abbey*. They were built as part of John Wood the Elder and Younger's plan to echo ancient Rome – Bath already had the Circus, and the Assembly Rooms were their equivalent of the Forum. After Wood the Elder died in 1754 it was left to his son to finish the neoclassical venue, which he did in 1771. There were four main rooms: the Ballroom, for the popular subscription dances held every season; the Tea or Concert Room; the Octagon Room, which linked the two major spaces; and a Card Room.

ABOVE
The Tea Room at the
Assembly Rooms –
one of the few places
you can't get tea in
Bath.

TOP RIGHT
Access to the
Assembly Rooms is
via a passageway
between Bennett
Street and Alfred
Street.

TOP RIGHT
Lady Danbury (Adjoa
Andoh) hosting the
ball where sparks fly
in Season One.

JANE AUSTEN

By the time Jane Austen stayed in Bath, between 1801 and 1805, the city was not quite as fashionable as it had been in the late 18th century, with Brighton becoming the new destination of choice. At that time there were two sets of assembly rooms: John Wood's 'Upper' or 'New' were up the hill close to his Royal Crescent and the Circus, while the 'Lower' assembly rooms were much older and located down in the town.

(They burned to the ground in 1820 and were not replaced.) Jane Austen notes in her diaries whether she attended the 'Upper rooms' or 'Lower rooms'. The Upper Assembly Rooms play a significant part in *Persuasion*; they are the setting for a pivotal scene in the story. The heroine, Anne Elliot, is eager to visit the Rooms in the hope of meeting her admirer, the Royal Navy's Captain Wentworth, but she is prevented by her father's snobbish attitude.

THE TEA ROOM AND BALLROOM

The Ballroom at the Assembly Rooms is the largest 18th-century room in Bath with its own musicians' gallery set above the dance floor. The high ceiling provided good ventilation on crowded ball nights when 800 people or more might attend, and perspiration was not to be countenanced for elegant young ladies. The windows set at a high level prevented outsiders from gazing in.

Bridgerton producers chose the smaller Tea Room next door as the location for Lady Danbury's Ball in Episode One. In Jane Austen's time it was used for both concerts and refreshments and was sometimes known as the Concert Room. During the evening entertainments there was an interval for tea, and dancers would adjourn from the ballroom and

gravitate to the ornate, galleried Tea Room.

In Georgian times, the Bath season of public balls ran from October to early June. The 'New' or 'Upper' Rooms held two balls a week; on Monday nights it was a Dress Ball and on Thursday nights a Fancy Ball. Subscriptions were offered for either ball at 14 shillings (70p/$1) during the 1815 season, which afforded the entrance to 28 balls in that time. Should you care to attend a ball for which you were *not* a subscriber, then the charge was a monstrous five shillings (25p/40c) for a single ball.

The Ballroom and Tea Room are linked by the equally grand Octagon Room with its four fireplaces and Gainsborough's portrait of the first Master of Ceremonies at the Upper Rooms, Captain William Wade. The Octagon Room was originally intended as a circulating space, but went on to host music recitals and card games. Today, the Assembly Rooms are run by the National Trust and under normal circumstances open for visitors.

BATH STREET & ALFRED STREET

Two of Bath's familiar streets are used in the opening sequence of Bridgerton

As *Bridgerton* begins we see the wide expanse of Alfred Street and good citizens in their Regency finery taking a stroll. Many elegant carriages are delivering 'ladies of precedence' to important social engagements across the city while Lady Whistledown begins her familiar voiceover. If this were Bath and not London, they would almost certainly be heading to the Assembly Rooms, which lie at the end of the street.

In Bath Street, more promenading takes place along a thoroughfare lined with classical colonnades and a view of the distant Cross Baths. It is down this street that our hero, Simon Basset, the newly anointed Duke of Hastings will ride, like some Regency Clint Eastwood arriving in town to settle his affairs.

Bath Street was built by Georgian Architect Thomas Baldwin in 1791,

along with the Cross Baths at the end of the street. This is where visitors can experience the healing properties of the water, which bubbles up at 46°C. Nearby is the famous Thermae Bath Spa, Britain's only natural thermal spa.

Each December Bath Street is one of the many streets lined with stalls for the annual Christmas Market, the perfect time for an out-of-season visit.

TOP LEFT AND RIGHT
Two views of Bath Street looking towards the Cross Baths at the end of the street. Behind the camera is the entrance to the ancient Roman Baths.

LEFT AND ABOVE
Two views of Alfred Street, with and without carriages.

GUNTER'S TEA SHOP

In London you'd find it in Berkeley Square – in Bath you'll find it at 12a Trim Street

Gunter's was a famous society tearoom catering to an upmarket clientele at 7–8 Berkeley Square in London. It had been started in 1757 by Domenico Negri, an Italian pastry cook, and he named his establishment The Pot and Pineapple. After the introduction of pineapples in the time of Charles II, the fruit had become a symbol of luxury and often used as the hallmark of confectioners engaged in the subtle art of sugar refining.

In 1777 Negri gained James Gunter as a partner, and the business flourished, producing a whole variety of 'sweetmeats' and ices. After Negri's death in 1799, Gunter decided to place his own name over the shop, but there was no diminution of trade.

In the early 19th century it effectively became England's first drive-in ice-cream parlour. The elite classes, out for a jaunt in the West End, would park up their carriages in Berkeley Square and waiters would ferry ice-creams out for them to eat in the comfort of their own conveyance.

Gunter encouraged his son Robert to study confectionery in Paris and the tea rooms were passed from generation to generation, only moving out in the mid-1930s when Berkeley Square was redeveloped. The new Gunter's tearoom in Curzon Street lasted until 1956.

Such was the cachet of Gunter's that for many years, when it was

ABOVE LEFT
A key plot moment between Daphne and Simon on the pavement outside Gunter's.

OPPOSITE
Bath's 18th-century stone street signs were set at first floor level so that carriage drivers could read them easily.

considered not correct for a lady to be seen alone with a gentleman at a place of refreshment in the afternoon, it was perfectly respectable for them to be seen at Gunter's Tea Shop. In Bath, the double-fronted shopfront at 12a Trim Street is home to Kimberly, a high-end fashion retailer, which gives us a bizarre *Bridgerton* twist. The Abbey Deli is a tea room made to look like a high-end fashion retailer; while Kimberly is a high-end fashion retailer adapted to be a tea room!

LEFT
No need to get the carriage out, Berkeley Square would have been just a short stroll from the Featheringtons and the Bridgertons in Grosvenor Square.

BELOW
No depiction of the original Pot and Pineapple/Gunter's survives, but cartoonist James Gillray satirised the obsession with confectioners in his 1797 cartoon 'Guard Duty at St. James's'.

ABOVE
The carriage comes to a halt after a run down Beauford Square.

RIGHT
'But which of your maids is married?' Eloise is shocked at Penelope's revelation.

CENTRE
Looking across Beauford Square at the 1805 Theatre Royal.

BEAUFORD SQUARE

When Bridgerton *characters are seen in transit, it's often in this picture-perfect Bath street*

Beauford Square was originally laid out by John Strahan in 1730, but today it is less of a square and more of a rectangle. In *Bridgerton* it is used as a regular thoroughfare and many carriage rides are taken up and down its short length while important issues are discussed.

On the north side of the square is a row of perfect Georgian terraced houses, while taking up the south side, and occupying some of the original square, is the Theatre Royal. Built in 1805 it was funded by a *Tontine* scheme with shares priced at £200. The Prince Regent, later to become George IV, was a subscriber, along with his brother the Duke of York and Albany. The sound of horses' hooves pounding along the cobbles of Beauford Square would have been familiar in the early 19th

century, as the original entrance to the theatre was via the Square.

In April 1862 a major fire gutted the interior of the building, taking everything in its path and leaving just the exterior walls standing. It was rebuilt with a new entrance on Saw Close, slap bang in front of the entrance to Beau Nash's House. This historic building was home to the unofficial 'King of Bath' who had been a prolific booster for the spa town in the 18th century and was the Master of Ceremonies at formal events. He died in 1761, handing over his duties to William Wade.

The iron railings surrounding the lawn on Beauford Square are original and were installed in 1805, supposedly to commemorate Admiral Nelson's victory at Trafalgar.

ABOVE
The age of the car is misleading. Philippa Savery took over the shop in 1946 and established an antiques business, often rescuing pieces from nearby buildings that were being 'improved'.

LEFT
Operated by the Landmark Trust, Elton House is beautifully furnished and can be rented out for short Bath stays.

THE ABBEY DELI

Where Daphne and Eloise buy their ball gowns, you can get a very familiar cup of tea…

The shop with bow-fronted windows on Abbey Street has a history that predates the starting point of *Bridgerton* by over a hundred years. Stand back a distance in Abbey Green and you can see it is part of Elton House, and the bones of the much-altered house date to 1699. Elizabeth and Jacob Elton bought the lease from the Duke of Kingston, enlarged the house and converted it into numerous lodgings. They were taking advantage of the Georgian fashion to take the waters at Bath, and Abbey Green was the fashionable centre of Bath, before it started shifting uphill towards the New Assembly Rooms.

Around 1800 the front of the building gained the shopfront, which sustained many businesses over the years, including a grocer's and a variety of cobblers. Elton House was still divided into 12 dwellings and a shop when Miss Philippa Savery moved in to sell antiques in 1946. Gradually, over time, as the residents died or moved on, she bought up the leases, until in 1962 she was able to buy the whole building and restore it to one property.

BELOW RIGHT
Two views of the shop at 2 Abbey Street.

BELOW
Lady Featherington and Marina pop in to Modiste for an accommodating new gown.

In 1982 she gave her life's work to the Landmark Trust, an organisation which rescues architecturally interesting buildings across the country, restores them and then rents them out on a short- or long-term basis. No.2 Abbey Street is preserved as a retail shop.

Since the antiques shop closed it has been home to a clothes shop, a bead shop, and ten years ago it became a café/delicatessen. With the sudden decline of tourist footfall during the Covid restrictions of 2020, the Pickled Greens deli closed, along with many famous Bath tea rooms nearby such as the Bath Bun and the Sally Lunn House.

Nicky and Jon Ison, who run delis in nearby Larkhall and Widcombe took it on in November 2020 and had little idea they were about to get global exposure, as Nicky Ison explains: 'The filming (for *Bridgerton*) was done during the Autumn of

the previous year, 2019. When we were considering the business we had no idea about the series. It was mentioned in passing that companies like to film as it's a pretty shop.'

Today, you can find Madame Delacroix's much-patronised premises behind Bath Abbey, and the Isons have big plans for a *Bridgerton*-themed room upstairs. 'It's a special room that is softer and quieter so afternoon tea can be taken away from the main shop's bustle. We are determined to keep our shop's integrity and still be a café and deli that offers home-baked foods rather than a Bridgerton Tourist Attraction or yet another "Regency tea room" – there are so many of these already in Bath and as local Bathonians we hope to try and cater for our local residents still.' Though with Lady Whistledown on the cushions and Modiste tea in the window, you can hardly avoid the connection.

ABOVE
The Abbey Deli can seat (under normal conditions and not distancing) around 50 people inside and 20 people outside.

LEFT
Looking down Abbey Street, towards Modiste, from the Abbey.

RIGHT
You won't find these on sale at Gunter's Tea Room.

ABBEY GREEN

One of Bath's oldest squares doubled as Covent Garden and the location for the Duke of Hastings' drunken night out

Tucked away behind Bath Abbey is an oasis of calm in what can be a crowded city at the height of the summer tourist season. Jane Austen moved out of Bath for the summer to avoid the heat, and beneath the branches of the giant London Plane tree, there is a large spread of welcome shade. Plane trees were popular city trees because of their non-invasive root system and the one in Abbey Green was planted in 1793.

Abbey Green, across York Street from the Abbey, is also close to the

Roman Baths and is the oldest part of the city. It was once a walled and gated courtyard to the Abbey Priory belonging to the Duke of Kingston who sold off leases to build on his land. Leading off the Green is North Parade Passage, which contains Bath's oldest house dating to 1482.

Abbey Green was used to depict the hustle and bustle of London's Covent Garden, such as the scene where Eloise picks out feathers while telling Penny her real ambition is to be an intelligent, independent woman like

ABOVE LEFT
The book shop at 5 Abbey Green, beyond the London Plane tree, was once the Abbeygate Tavern.

OPPOSITE
The Crystal Palace public house is on the original site of 10/11 Abbey Green, which previously had been lodging houses. Lord Nelson stayed there on one of his frequent visits to Bath. There is also an excellent Nelson Trail visitors can follow.

LEFT
The Columbian coffee shop disappeared behind a stage set for Simon's night on the town.

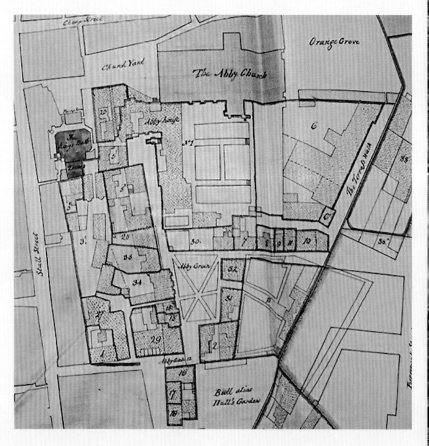

Lady Whistledown. Modiste couturier is just a few yards up the road, and so the Green can be seen when Lord Bridgerton comes looking for Siena at the house next door to Modiste, or when Eloise at last thinks she knows the identity of Lady Whistledown.

Location manager Paul Tomlinson explained that his life was made a lot easier by the residents: 'Abbey Green deserves a special mention due to the amount of work that was undertaken to achieve our filming. In order to film those scenes we had to reach agreements with all the surrounding shops so we could cover any modern aspects of their buildings with period dressing. This involved liaising with over 50 individual properties so we could carry out our works while keeping disruption to a minimum.'

Indeed, for the scene where Will Mondrich discovers a drunken Duke of Hastings slumped underneath the Abbeygate Arch (it's a relatively recent arch, the old Abbey Gate is long gone), a whole new façade was placed in front of the Columbian Coffee Company.

Had the Duke been indulging in a pub crawl in the 19th century he would have found two public houses within a few steps of where he was lying down. The Raven Inn/Bladud's Head/Freemason's Tavern (now Black's outdoor equipment) dates from the 18th century. In 1851 the police wanted it closed down because it opened on Sunday mornings and 'allowed prostitutes and other bad characters to resort to them'.

OPPOSITE
An early map of Bath Abbey and the Priory land shows Abbey Green and the Roman Baths in blue, but York Street is yet to be built.

LEFT
Stalls set up on Abbey Green to represent Covent Garden, awaiting the arrival of the supporting artists and film crew. Author Julia Quinn visited the set to watch these scenes being recorded.

BELOW
Abbey Green looking past the Crystal Palace on the right towards Abbeygate Street in the 1920s. The arch across the road was only built in 1973.

BATH GUILDHALL

Location of one of Bridgerton's many authentic Georgian ballrooms

Before he built Bath Street, architect Thomas Baldwin designed the Bath Guildhall, which was constructed between 1775 and 1778, just across the road from Bath Abbey. A central dome and the north and south wings were added in 1893, accommodating an indoor market on the site that is still open today.

There are council chambers, a banqueting suite, and one of the grandest features of the building is the ballroom, which is often used for events during the Bath International Music Festival. *Bridgerton* producers used the ballroom in Episode Three where Daphne and the Duke dance

their way carefully around a table of glasses in the middle of the room.

LE BEAU MONDE

Despite many years waging war against France, the French language was very popular in England during the Regency, as were French fashion and furniture. Le Beau Monde was a name given to English high society, and another French derivative came to be used – 'ton'. The word 'ton' is derived from *haut ton*, or high tone, and refers to the fashionable elite. They exhibited the refined manners which characterised those of good breeding and wealth. They represented the top echelon of society

which was able to live in luxury without vocation and spent most of their time pursuing pleasure.

THE RULES OF BATH

Master of Ceremonies for the town, Beau Nash, set strict social rules for those attending balls in Bath and they were reinforced by his successor William Wade. On October 1, 1771, the start of the Season, he announced: 'It being absolutely necessary, that a propriety of dress should be observed at so polite an assembly as that of Bath, it is humbly requested of the company to comply with the following regulations:

• That ladies who dance minuets be dressed in a suit of clothes, or a full-trimmed sack, with lappets and dressed hoops, such as are usually worn at St James's.

• It is requested of those ladies who do not dance minuets, not to take up the front seats at the balls.

• That no lady dance country-dances in a hoop of any kind and those who choose to pull their hoops off, will be assisted by proper servants in an apartment for that purpose.

• That gentlemen who dance minuets, do wear a full-trimmed suit of clothes.

• Officers in the navy or army in their uniforms are desired to wear their hair or wig *en queue* (tied with a ribbon).

• Ladies are not to appear with hats, nor gentlemen with boots, in an evening, after the balls are begun.'

BELOW LEFT AND OPPOSITE
Two views of the Guildhall ballroom, which, like its Assembly Rooms equivalent, has a musicians' gallery to keep the dance floor unencumbered. Except when set designers place a table full of glasses in the centre...

BELOW
The exterior of Bath Guildhall.

HOLBURNE MUSEUM OF ART

GREAT PULTENEY STREET

It started life as the Sydney Hotel and took on a new life as Lady Danbury's mansion

Bath in the late 1790s was still a fashionable and cultured city, attracting writers, musicians and intellectuals. Keen to rival London, which had its own Vauxhall Pleasure Gardens (recreated in Episode One of *Bridgerton*), Bath set about laying out one of its own. The Sydney Gardens, also known as Bath Vauxhall Gardens, were opened in 1795 across the River Avon from the town in an area developed by Sir William Pulteney as 'Bathwick'. It was a commercial pleasure garden of ten acres with a maze, grotto, sham castle and, in 1810, a mechanised model village with flowing water known as 'The Cascade'. By night the gardens were illuminated with over

15,000 'variegated lamps' to limit the temptation of scandalous goings-on, such as ladies walking with gentlemen unaccompanied.

The foundation stone of the Sydney Hotel was laid in 1796 and the building was opened to the public in 1799. As can be seen from the 1805 painting by J. C. Nattes (on page 32), projecting from the rear of the building at first-floor level was a semi-circular orchestra stand. Two semi-circular rows of dining stalls projected from the sides of the building at ground-floor level for diners to enjoy the music drifting down from above. They could also gaze out upon the many promenaders. Jane Austen often

visited during her time in Bath and enjoyed the public breakfasts, which included the local speciality, the Sally Lunn bun. Sydney Gardens provided her favourite walk, as the family had rented rooms at 4 Sydney Place, facing out over the pleasure gardens.

Although tourism was boosted by the arrival of the Great Western Railway in 1840, the Sydney Hotel had already failed and was converted into private lodgings in 1836. From 1853 until 1880 it became the Bath Proprietary College, and was almost demolished and replaced with a five-storey Victorian hotel after that. However, the site's distance from the station and the city centre counted against it, and when the enormous Empire Hotel was built in Orange Grove, close to Bath Abbey, the building plans were shelved.

It lay derelict until the trustees of the Holburne Museum acquired it in 1913 and restored the building for use as an exhibition space, opening to the public in June 1916. Over a century later, the Holburne is still displaying Sir William's lifetime collection of fine art, including paintings, porcelain and sculptures. The most dramatic addition came in 2011 with an £11 million, three-story extension grafted onto the rear of the building looking out onto Sydney Gardens.

ABOVE
A classic painting of the Sydney Hotel viewed from the Pleasure Gardens, by J. C. Nattes.

RIGHT
The Holburne's modern extension gave the museum much-needed extra space.

RIGHT
No sooner had it been built than modern transport divided the park. The Kennet & Avon Canal Company paid 2,000 guineas to pass through the gardens via two short tunnels and under two cast-iron footbridges. Cleveland House is the former headquarters of the Kennet & Avon Canal Company. A trap-door in the tunnel roof was used to pass paperwork between clerks above and bargees below.

PICKLED GREENS

No. 2

LOCATION REPORT

Filming in one of Britain's most popular tourist cities presented its own problems – but no one batted an eyelid at the Regency costumes

When Chris Van Dusen and Shonda Rhimes put together their ideal list of Georgian shooting locations there were only four realistic choices – Edinburgh's New Town, Cheltenham, Dublin or Bath. All these cities have a wealth of Georgian architecture which would act as a perfect backdrop to the drama. With many of the other key locations being in London and the South of England (see our companion title *Bridgerton's England* for the full inventory) and for the level of architectural preservation (it is a UNESCO World Heritage City), Bath was the obvious choice. Location manager Paul Tomlinson explained to *Bath Life* magazine that the golden Bath stone also gave a brightness to scenes that complemented the

ABOVE
Phoebe Dynevor waits for her scene outside Modiste in some non-Regency Uggs, while a kindly crew member protects the hair.

RIGHT
Some of the best-dressed supporting artists gather on the pavement in the Royal Crescent.

production designers' vivid colour palette used for costumes in the drama.

Once the decision to film in Bath had been made, the production team approached the Bath Film Office to help arrange permissions to close streets and shoot on council-owned property. Their advice to location managers was, 'avoid filming at the peak of the tourist season in July and August'. Thanks to its Roman baths, the Abbey, the many museums and the long association with Jane Austen, Bath is a top tourist destination. Unfortunately, due to 'unforeseen circumstances' one of the team's visits had to be in August 2019. But they coped.

A film unit that needs to close roads and restrict access needs six to eight weeks' advance notice, but in the case of *Bridgerton* a team of people started work five months ahead of shooting because of the sheer number of properties involved. For a start, over half of the residences in Royal Crescent needed to be ticked off the list, as well as the homes and businesses on Alfred Street, Beauford Square, Trim Street, Bath Street and Abbey Green.

Production in Bath was a massive undertaking with up to two hundred in the crew, and in addition to the main cast members there could be anything up to a hundred extras on set. So the film crew set up an operations base at Bath Racecourse, above the town, where the majority of the costume, make-up and technical trailers could be parked, with the actors bussed into town. There was a separate equestrian facility in the large Charlotte Street car park (directly downhill from the Royal Crescent and Royal Avenue). The production team also established 'horse routes' through the city to keep disruption to a minimum. One of the pivotal scenes, where Lady Danbury explains to the Duke of Hastings that he should not let Daphne waste her opportunity

with Prince Friedrich, was filmed in the Royal Crescent. However, getting horses and carriages to Abbey Street and Abbey Green meant a trip into the heart of tourist Bath near the Abbey.

Filming in such venerable locations had its own limitations, as Paul Tomlinson explained: 'Most of the locations were in or around listed buildings, which means a great deal of care had to be taken to protect the fabric of the buildings and make sure no damage was caused during our filming. This often meant preparatory works took longer than normal given the extra care required. Thankfully we had a very respectful crew who treated all the locations with a great deal of care.'

Given that Julia Quinn's novels follow on from the literary tradition

established by Jane Austen, it was fitting that *Bridgerton* filmed in locations she would have known, such as Sydney Gardens, the Royal Crescent and the Assembly Rooms.

'I really enjoyed our filming at the Bath Assembly Rooms,' Paul explained, 'which feature a set of original chandeliers that were made

TOP
Horses waiting to get hitched outside the No.1 Royal Crescent Museum.

ABOVE
Short-term parking for a Featherington family coach, with its butterfly insignia.

RIGHT
One of the supporting artists in coachman's attire makes his way to the set. *Bridgerton*'s crew were surprised at how little notice the public took of extras in Regency garb, but in a city famed for its Jane Austen Festival and museum staff in period dress, it is a familiar occurrence.

BELOW
A coach with the Hastings crest emblazoned on the door is prepared for a run along Beauford Square.

for the building in 1771. They're considered one of the finest sets to have survived from the 18th century and were described to us as "irreplaceable". We wanted to feature the chandeliers in our filming as they added to the beauty of the location, which involved lowering them so they would appear within our shots, and using a camera crane so the camera could pass above the chandeliers looking down at the dancers below. I was very relieved once we had finished our filming and the chandeliers were raised back to their normal height!'

 # WILTON HOUSE

Only 36 miles from Bath, Wilton House plays many leading roles in Bridgerton

One moment it's Hyde park, the next it's St James's Palace, but the North Front of Wilton House is probably the most recognisable of all Wilton House's guises, as the exterior of the Duke of Hastings' London residence. It has been the actual home of the earls of Pembroke for over 400 years,

from the 1st Earl, William Herbert, to the 18th Earl, William Herbert, who inherited the title in 2005 at the tender age of 25.

Wilton had come into the family thanks to a bit of religious robbery. The 1st Earl married Anne Parr, the

sister of Catherine Parr, who was to become the sixth (and surviving) wife of Henry VIII. After marrying Catherine, Henry ennobled William Herbert and gave him the former monastery as a gift. Four hundred years later, for tax inheritance purposes, the estate is now a charitable trust and the earl pays rent on the third of the house that he lives in.

Wilton House is famous for its magnificent art collection and there are no finer paintings than those found in the Double Cube Room, which in the 17th century was known as 'the Great Dining Roome'. The

LEFT
Before the Hastings' ball in the final episode of Series One, the camera sweeps down from a similar aerial view into the courtyard.

BELOW
Simon and Daphne contemplate the future before the final ball of the Season.

BELOW LEFT
If the Featheringtons stood aside, we could see the famous Holbein Porch that was once attached to the house, but was moved to the end of a walkway during a critically panned renovation by the 11th Earl. Meanwhile, Colin has an announcement...

grand state room was designed by England's leading architect, Inigo Jones, to showcase the family's large collection of paintings by Anthony Van Dyck. It is his expansive painting of the 4th Earl and his family which hangs behind Queen Charlotte in *Bridgerton* as she scrutinises the young ladies from distinguished families being presented at court. The

French windows look out to the River Nadder – and centred across from them is a large white marble fireplace.

Fans of period drama may recognise the Double Cube Room from Keira Knightley's *Pride and Prejudice*, or from *The Crown*, and in *Outlander* it stood in for the Palace of Versailles. Elsewhere, the estate grounds, with

ABOVE
The Featheringtons' big moment approaches. Can Penelope, Prudence and Philippa keep their cool under the gimlet eye of Her Majesty?

a beautiful 250-year-old cedar of Lebanon, are used to portray Hyde Park where Daphne goes riding with her bother Lord Bridgerton, and she and the Duke of Hastings have a morning promenade along the chalk stream of the River Nadder.

Less recognizsable is the formal parterre garden in front of the old pavilion at Wilton. This is the setting for Colin's surprise announcement that he and Marina are engaged to be married, which comes with both shock and surprise to their respective families.

BELOW
The height of embellishment, Inigo Jones' famous Double Cube Room. The Herberts have scratched around and bought a bigger rug now.

RIGHT
One of the cloistered corridors at Wilton seen in the series, such as when Simon's mother, the Duchess of Hastings, is in labour.

BRIDGERTON WALKING TOUR

All the sites mentioned in the book are detailed in the map on the back cover. This route starts at the top of the town, and it's downhill all the way. However, Bath has so many interesting diversions it might take a strong discipline to stick to the plan

1. ROYAL CRESCENT

We start our Bridgerton Walking Tour at the Royal Crescent – scene of many carriage rides, galloping horses and Lord Bridgerton's final plea to Siena Rosso. For those travelling to Bath by car there is a large, open car park just below the Crescent in Charlotte Street (with a pedestrian cut-through in the north-west corner – you can just about see it in the aerial photo on P.6) alternatively there is metered parking on Royal Avenue. Parasols and silver-topped walking canes at the ready, we start at No.30, and enjoy a promenade around John Wood the Younger's masterpiece till we get to No.1.

2. NO.1 ROYAL CRESCENT

No.1 Royal Crescent Museum is the façade of the Featherington's Grosvenor Square mansion, but thanks to clever CGI, the view on screen has buildings to its left, rather than the cobbled Royal Crescent curving away. The location crew were able to place lions and lampposts outside, while the balcony was a CGI addition. Take a tour round a genuine Georgian-furnished house or carry on down Brock Street to John Wood the Elder's impressive Circus and take the north pavement to Bennett Street. Fifty metres or so down Bennett Street, the plaza of the Assembly Rooms opens up downhill to your right.

3. THE ASSEMBLY ROOMS

The Assembly Rooms are an important venue in the world of Jane Austen and are administered by the National Trust. Lady Danbury held her ball in the Tea Room and, like No.1 Museum, it can be viewed for an entrance fee. Once perused, continue on down the hill and turn left into Alfred Street.

4. ALFRED STREET

Alfred Street makes its entrance very early in *Bridgerton* as one of the scene-setting streets of London.

OPPOSITE
Bath Abbey viewed through the York Street archway. Keep going and turn right for Abbey Street and Abbey Green.

RIGHT
The back of the Theatre Royal looms over Beauford Square.

Take a quick glimpse before heading downhill along the Bartlett Street passageway till you get to George Street. Turn right and go straight to the end of George Street then head downhill along Gay Street to the bottom of Queen Square. Take a left along Wood Street/Northumberland Buildings, and then it's first right, downhill once more, into Queen Street. At the bottom you will see an elegant archway. Beyond that archway is Trim Street. Turn left and head towards No.12a.

5. TRIM STREET

Trim Street is home to Gunter's Tea Rooms. To minimise disruption in the city, the *Bridgerton* team chose locations where there was a minimum of through-traffic. There are some beautiful Georgian shops throughout Bath, but many of the best are on impossibly busy streets. At the far end of Trim Street, at No.12a, you will find the shopfront used for Gunter's tea room. Then it's about-face: head back down Trim Street, cross Barton Street and you are in Beauford Square.

6. BEAUFORD SQUARE

Beauford Square is a perfect backdrop for many carriage rides, with its perfect Georgian houses on one side and the back of the 1805 Theatre Royal on the other. Take a stroll down and back, past 'Dolly' the bulldog, if she's out, and then it's back to Barton Street and a right turn.

Still heading downhill, Barton Street becomes Saw Close and you pass the house of Bath grandee Beau Nash (he must have got the 'Beau' very early on) to the right, slap bang next to the entrance to the Theatre Royal. Further down the hill is a complicated junction, but you need to head straight on down Westgate, which has a bus stop on the right. Just past the bus stop turn left down a passageway that leads to the Cross Baths and Bath Street. If you miss that turning off Westgate there's another passageway a little further along on the left.

7. CROSS BATHS AND BATH STREET

Bath Street, like Alfred Street, is a good scene-setting street where the latest Whistledown can be purchased and where Simon Basset makes his entrance to the drama. Head down the colonnaded street towards the entrance to the Roman Baths, (the backdrop to Regé-Jean Page's farewell tweet) then take a quick right and left into York Street, which has a beautiful arch across the road and runs parallel to the Abbey. Less than a hundred metres down York Street take a right turn into Abbey Street.

8. ABBEY DELI

Instantly reconisable as Modiste, the Abbey Deli, is the perfect place to rest awhile and try out some of the specialist infusions on the menu. It's also a chance to look at the Queen Anne-era wood panelling, one of the few *Bridgerton* interiors filmed in Bath. Suitably refreshed, it's out of the

TOP
The beautiful Pulteney Bridge across the River Avon.